Starting with...
Role play

At the shops

Diana Bentley

Maggie Hutchings

Dee Reid

Diana Bentley is an educational consultant for primary literacy and has written extensively for both teachers and children. She worked for many years in the Centre for the Teaching of Reading at Reading University and then became a Senior Lecturer in Primary English at Oxford Brookes University. Throughout her professional life she has continued to work in schools and teach children aged from 5 to 11 years.

Maggie Hutchings has considerable experience teaching KS1 and Early Years. She is a Leading Teacher for literacy in The Foundation Stage and is a Foundation Stage and Art coordinator. Maggie is passionate about the importance of learning through play and that learning should be an exciting and fun experience for young children. Her school's art work has been exhibited in The National Gallery, London.

Dee Reid is a former teacher who has been an independent consultant in primary literacy for over 20 years in many local authorities. She is consultant to 'Catch Up' – a special needs literacy intervention programme used in over 4,000 schools in the UK. She is Series Consultant to 'Storyworlds' (Heinemann) and her recent publications include 'Think About It' (Nelson Thornes) and Literacy World (Heinemann).

Other titles in the series:

Colour and light
Under the ground
Emergency 999
Into space
At the hospital
Fairytales
At the garage/At the airport
All creatures great and small
On the farm
Water
Ourselves

Other Foundation titles:

Starting with stories and poems:

Self esteem
Self care
A sense of community
Making relationships
Behaviour and self control

A collection of stories and poems

Starting with our bodies and movement

Starting with sounds and letters

The authors would like to thank Jane Whitwell for all her hard work in compiling the resources and poems for the series.

Published by
Hopscotch Educational Publishing Ltd, Unit 2, The Old Brushworks, 56 Pickwick Road, Corsham, Wiltshire, SN13 9BX
Tel: 01249 701701

© 2006 Hopscotch Educational Publishing

Written by Diana Bentley, Maggie Hutchings and Dee Reid
Series design by Blade Communications
Cover illustration by Sami Sweeten
Illustrated by Susan Hutchison
Printed by Colorman (Ireland) Ltd

ISBN 1 905390 11 4

Diana Bentley, Maggie Hutchings and Dee Reid hereby assert their moral right to be identified as the authors of this work in accordance with the Copyright, Designs and Patents Act, 1988.

The authors and publisher would like to thank Chapter One (a specialist children's book shop) in Wokingham for all their help and support. Email: chapteronebookshop@yahoo.co.uk

Contents

Acknowledgements

The authors and publisher gratefully acknowledge permission to reproduce copyright material in this book.

'Shopping Basket' by Charles Thomson from *A Red Poetry Paintbox* compiled by John Foster (Oxford University Press) © 1994 Charles Thomson. Reproduced by kind permission of the author.

'If I were Father Christmas' by Richard Edwards. © Richard Edwards. Reproduced by kind permission of the author.

'Christmas' by Brenda Williams from *My First Christmas Poems* compiled by John Foster (Oxford University Press) © Brenda Williams. Reproduced by kind permission of the author.

Every effort has been made to trace the owners of copyright of material in this book and the publisher apologises for any inadvertent omissions. Any persons claiming copyright for any material should contact the publisher who will be happy to pay the permission fees agreed between them and who will amend the information in this book on any subsequent reprint.

Introduction

There are 12 books in the series *Starting with role play* offering a complete curriculum for the Early Years.

Ourselves	*At the garage/At the airport*
Into space	*Emergency 999*
At the shops	*All creatures great and small*
Colour and light	*Under the ground*
At the hospital	*Fairytales*
On the farm	*Water*

While each topic is presented as a six-week unit of work, it can easily be adapted to run for fewer weeks if necessary. The themes have been carefully selected to appeal to boys and girls and to a range of cultural groups.

 Each unit addresses all six areas of learning outlined in the *Curriculum Guidance for the Foundation Stage* and the specific Early Learning Goal is identified for each activity and indicated by this symbol.

Generally, differentiation is achieved by outcome, although for some of the Communication, Language and Literacy strands and Mathematical Development strands, extension activities are suggested for older or more confident learners.

Suggested teaching sequence for each unit

Each week has been organised into a suggested teaching sequence. However, each activity in an area of learning links to other activities and there will be overlap as groups engage with the tasks.

The Core Curriculum: Literacy and Mathematics

Every school will have its own programmes for literacy and mathematics and it is not intended that the activities in the units in this book should replace these. Rather, the activities suggested aim to support any programme, to help to consolidate the learning and to demonstrate how the learning can be used in practical situations.

The importance of role play

'Children try out their most recent learning, skills and competences when they play. They seem to celebrate what they know.'

Tina Bruce (2001) Learning Through Play: Babies, Toddlers and the Foundation Years. London: Hodder & Stoughton.

Early Years practitioners are aware of the importance of play as a vehicle for learning. When this play is carefully structured and managed then the learning opportunities are greatly increased. Adult participation can be the catalyst for children's imaginations and creativity.

Six weeks allows for a role play area to be created, developed and expanded and is the optimum time for inspiring children and holding their interest. It is important not to be too prescriptive in the role play area. Teachers should allow for children's ideas and interests to evolve and allow time for the children to explore and absorb information. Sometimes, the children will take the topic off at a tangent or go into much greater depth than expected or even imagined.

Organising the classroom

The role play area could be created by partitioning off a corner of the classroom with ceiling drapes, an old-style clothes-horse, chairs, boxes, large-scale construction blocks (for example, 'Quadro') or even an open-fronted beach tent/shelter. Alternatively, the whole classroom could be dedicated to the role play theme.

Involving parents and carers

Encourage the children to talk about the topic and what they are learning with their parents or carers at home. With adult help and supervision, they can explore the internet and search for pictures in magazines and books. This enriches the learning taking place in the classroom.

Outside activities

The outdoor classroom should be an extension of the indoor classroom and it should support and enhance the activities offered inside. Boys, in particular, often feel less restricted in outdoor play. They may use language more purposefully and may even engage more willingly in reading and writing activities. In the outdoor area things can be done on a much bigger, bolder and noisier scale and this may connect with boys' preferred learning styles.

Observation in Salford schools and settings noted that boys access books much more readily when there is a book area outdoors.

Resources

Role play areas can be more convincing reconstructions when they are stocked with authentic items. Car boot sales, jumble sales and charity shops are good sources of artefacts. It is a good idea to inform parents and carers of topics well in advance so they can be looking out for objects and materials that will enhance the role play area.

Reading

Every week there should be a range of opportunities for children to participate in reading experiences. These should include:

Shared reading

The practitioner should read aloud to the children from Big Books, modelling the reading process; for example, demonstrating that print is read from left to right. Shared reading also enables the practitioner to draw attention to high frequency words, the spelling patterns of different words and punctuation. Where appropriate, the practitioner should cover words and ask the children to guess which word would make sense in the context. This could also link with phonic work where the children could predict the word based on seeing the initial phoneme. Multiple readings of the same text enable them to become familiar with story language and tune in to the way written language is organised into sentences.

Independent reading

As children become more confident with the written word they should be encouraged to recognise high frequency words. Practitioners should draw attention to these words during shared reading and shared writing. Children should have the opportunity to read these words in context and to play word matching and word recognition games. Encourage the children to use their ability to hear the sounds at various points in words and to use their knowledge of those phonemes to decode simple words.

Writing

Shared writing

Writing opportunities should include teacher demonstration, teacher scribing, copy writing and independent writing. (Suggestions for incorporating shared writing are given each week.)

Emergent writing

The role play area should provide ample opportunities for children to write purposefully, linking their writing with the task in hand. These meaningful writing opportunities help children to understand more about the writing process and to seek to communicate in writing. Children's emergent writing should occur alongside their increasing awareness of the 'correct' form of spellings. In the example below, the child is beginning to have an understanding of letter shapes as well as the need to write from left to right.

Assessment

When children are actively engaged in the role play area this offers ample opportunities for practitioners to undertake observational assessments. By participating in the role play area the practitioner can take time to talk in role to the children about their work and assess their performance. The assessment grid on page 36 enables practitioners to record progress through the appropriate Stepping Stone or Early Learning Goal.

DfES publications

The following publications will be useful:

Progression in Phonics (DfES 0178/2000)
Developing Early Writing (DfES 0055/2001)
Playing with Sounds (DfES 0280/2004)

At the shops	Role play area	Personal, Social and Emotional Development	Communication, Language and Literacy	Knowledge and Understanding of the World	Mathematical Development	Creative Development	Physical Development
Week 1	Building the supermarket	*Sustain attentive listening* Talking about knowledge of shops and shopping experiences	*Hear and say initial and final sounds in words* Sharing rhymes Writing labels for people who work in shops	*Identify features of where they live* Discussing pictures of shops and supermarkets Asking questions	*Count reliably* Identifying fruit and vegetables and counting items Introduce 1p coins	*Use imagination in art and design* Building the supermarket area Making fruit/vegetables Making collage frieze	*Move with control and coordination* Miming they are going shopping – dramatising visit
Week 2	Making things to buy and sell	*Respond to significant experiences* Discussing being lost	*Use talk to organise and clarify thinking* Playing 'What is it?' Writing shopping lists	*Investigate objects using senses* Removing labels from cans What happens when we don't know the contents?	*Solve practical problems using maths* Talking about cans and discovering how to stack them Drawing pattern of cans	*Communicate ideas through wide range of materials* Looking at bar codes Creating own bar codes Making lorries to deliver to the supermarket	*Move with confidence and imagination* Playing beans game
Week 3	Making bread for the bakery	*Be confident to try new activities* Asking questions Exploring 'sales talk'	*Enjoy using spoken and written language* Listening to non-fiction book Following instructions	*Identify things they like/dislike* Looking at advertisements Looking at changes when food is cooked	*Use vocabulary of adding and subtracting* Introduce 5p coins Encourage buying, using various coins	*Explore texture, shape and form* Making items to sell in the bakery	*Handle tools and malleable materials* Using salt dough to demonstrate changing shapes Playing beans game
Week 4	Being scientists and solving problems	*Be aware of own needs and views of others* Talking about turn taking	*Write ... simple sentences* Making 'lift-the-flap' book with the class Making own book about what they want to buy	*Assemble and join materials* Making bag to carry tin of beans Making vehicle to carry apples to supermarket	*Use mathematical ideas to solve practical problems* Adding and subtracting using 10p coins Estimating quantities	*Use imagination in drama* Creating tableau Taking photographs Dramatising situation in supermarket	*Show awareness of space* Playing shopping game
Week 5	Visiting the toy shop	*Have respect for own culture and that of others* Telling the Christmas story Discussing giving	*Explore and experiment with sounds, words, texts* Listening to story Writing notices for shop Using language to express ideas about giving	*Find out about environment* Discussing shopping at Christmas time	*Recognise and create simple patterns* Programming Roamer Making sequential pattern	*Explore colour, shape and texture* Making a toy shop Wrapping gifts Making toys Making 3-D Christmas cards	*Move with control and coordination* Moving as if on shopping trip Taking a walk to Bethlehem
Week 6	Visiting Father Christmas in his grotto	*Respond to significant experiences* Talking about excitement Talking about people who might be lonely at Christmas Making a Christmas wish	*Write for different purposes* Writing letter to Father Christmas Singing rhyming songs	*Find out about features in the place they live* Looking at different Christmas trees and decorations	*Solve practical problems* Wrapping up some parcels Placing boxes inside a large box	*Use imagination in art and design* Making calendars Designing stamps Making decorations Decorating grotto Making gifts	*Handle tools safely* Cutting out shapes Dramatising visit of Father Christmas Playing 'Father Christmas brings a present'

In this six-week unit, the children will be investigating shops and shopping. The role play area will start off as a supermarket, which will then be converted into a toy shop, ready for Christmas. For the first four weeks' talk and play will revolve around going to the supermarket, buying and selling, and taking on the roles of customer and shop assistant. If possible, try to arrange a visit to a supermarket over the course of the unit. In the last two weeks, role play will focus on Christmas celebrations and the children can dress up as Father Christmas and talk about giving and receiving.

Resource the dressing-up box with suitable costumes for mums, dads, shop assistants (in the same shirts or blouses), the manager and babies. In Week 6 you will need a Father Christmas costume (old dressing gown, tunic or hat).

By the end of the unit children will have:

- drawn a plan of a supermarket
- created shelves, aisles and stands to display the goods
- drawn and painted pictures of lorries and made a delivery lorry
- made paper fruit and vegetables for the supermarket
- made a collage frieze of a shop scene
- baked bread for the bread counter
- made Christmas decorations
- made a toy for the toy shop
- created a calendar
- made Christmas biscuits.

WEEK 1

Starting the role play area

This week, the role play area will become a supermarket. Over the course of the week, in Creative Development the children will plan and build the supermarket. They will make fruit and vegetables to display on the **shelves** and write **labels**. They will go into the supermarket and take on roles such as the customer, the assistant at the till, the shelf stacker and the manager. As they enter the supermarket, the children should find and wear their name badges and labels to indicate their role.

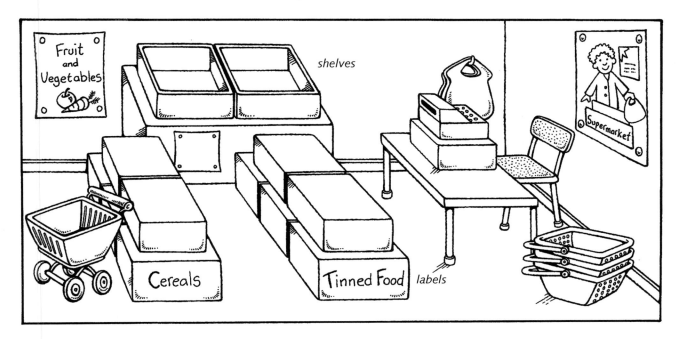

Resources

Photocopiable:

Poems and songs 1 (page 30)

Fiction books:

Don't forget the bacon by Pat Hutchings, Red Fox (0 099413 98 1)
Teddybears go Shopping by Susanna Gretz, A&C Black
(0 713653 60 4)
Going Shopping by Sarah Garland, Puffin (0 140554 00 9)

Non-fiction books:

Going Shopping by Pippa Goodhart and Brita Granstrom,
Franklin Watts (0 749646 82 9)
Who helps us … in the Supermarket, 'Little Nippers' series,
Heinemann Library (0 431173 23 0)

Music and songs:

Tom Thumb's Musical Maths by Helen MacGregor, A&C Black
(0 713649 71 2)

Materials:

- A number of large cardboard boxes to form the display shelves and units
- Pictures or photographs of shops, if possible in the local environment
- Pictures of fruit and vegetables, or real ones if possible
- Two containers labelled 'fruit' and 'vegetables'
- Two large card circles (approximate diameter 46cm) labelled 'fruit' and 'vegetables' with appropriate picture on each
- Paper cut into basket shapes in four colours (red, green, brown, orange)
- Frieze paper
- Crepe paper – reds, orange, white, greens and browns
- Newspaper
- 1p coins
- Various purses
- Materials for collage – beads, pieces of fabric and pictures of shops, food and people from magazines

Personal, Social and Emotional Development

 Sustain attentive listening, responding to what they have heard by relevant comments, questions or actions.

Introduce the topic

- ❑ Brainstorm with the children their knowledge and experiences of shops and shopping. Ask them to describe a shopping trip they have been on. Ask the following questions: Can you remember the name of the shops you visited? What did you buy?
- ❑ Tell the children that they are going to create their own supermarket in the role play area.
- ❑ Brainstorm ideas for products to sell in the supermarket and the people who would be working in it. Decide on a limited range of products – bread and cakes, fruit and vegetables, canned foods and breakfast cereals.

Circle time

- ❑ Ask the children if they like going shopping. Which shops do they like best? What happens if they want something from a shop that they can't have?

Knowledge and Understanding of the World

 Observe, find out about and identify features in the place they live and the natural world.

Different shops

- ❑ Look at pictures and photographs of different shops and discuss them with the class – for example, the window display and the name of the shop. Ask the children what they think the shops would look like inside and what they could buy in these shops.
- ❑ Show a picture of a supermarket and discuss its size and the huge variety of things to buy all under one roof.
- ❑ Ask the children the following questions: What do you put your shopping in? What are the people who work in shops called? What jobs do they do? What are the people who buy things called? Can you tell me the names of different types of shops

and what they might sell? (Supermarket, toy shop, butcher's, baker's, florist's, newsagent's, book shop and so on)

Creative Development

 Use their imagination in art and design.

Building the supermarket

- ❑ Ask a group of children to design the layout of the aisles on frieze paper. They should, with supervision, work cooperatively, talk about their ideas and negotiate. Using their design, place the cardboard boxes to make the aisles and checkout.
- ❑ Discuss with the children what products will be displayed on the shelves in each aisle and report back to the class.
- ❑ Ask all the children to draw and colour with felt-tipped pens an item to stick on the appropriate shelf. Add labels between aisles (see Communication, Language and Literacy).

Making the fruit and vegetables

- ❑ Look at pictures of real fruit and vegetables. Ask the children to scrunch newspaper to make a ball the size of a fruit or vegetable. Provide some ready-cut crepe paper and strips of adhesive tape (stuck on the table edge). Tell the children to select the most appropriate colour and cover the newspaper. More able children could attempt sealing their work with more tape. Do this for younger or less able children. (NB: completely covering the crepe paper with adhesive tape ensures strength and durability.)
- ❑ To make a cucumber, roll newspaper and cover with green crepe paper. Pull into shape with adhesive tape.

- ❑ To make a leek, graduate the colour from white to green. Extend the crepe paper at the top and snip the end.
- ❑ To make a cabbage or cauliflower, cover a ball of newspaper, as above, then add leaves of green crepe paper.

Making a collage frieze

- ❑ Give the children a piece of paper and ask them to draw a picture of somebody in a shop – for example, pushing a trolley, carrying a basket, reaching up to a high shelf or bending down to a low shelf. Ask them to paint their people and cut them out. Encourage them to add other collage materials such as beads for a necklace or pieces of fabric and cut-out pictures from magazines to stick in the trolley or basket. Stick these pictures onto the frieze paper and display in the role play area.

Mathematical Development

 Be able to count reliably. Use developing mathematical ideas and methods to solve practical problems.

Sorting

- ❑ Show the children the two large circles of card labelled 'fruit' and 'vegetables'. Make sure that they can identify which is which (the picture on each will help non-readers). Sort the fruits and vegetables (see Creative Development) by asking the children to place them on the appropriate circle. Count the fruits. Count the vegetables. Ask the children if there are more fruits than vegetables.
- ❑ Show the children basket shapes of paper in green, brown, orange and red. Ask them to sort the fruit and vegetables by colour by placing them on the appropriate basket.
- ❑ Ask the children to count and sort the fruit and vegetables and to put them into the two labelled containers in the role play area.

Extension

- ❑ Help the children to create number sums to represent the fruit and vegetables in the labelled circles; for example, 5 apples + 4 oranges = 9 fruits.

Counting

- In the role play area, introduce 1p coins. Show the children how to write '1p', '2p' up to '10p'. Make price labels for the fruits and vegetables and stick them to the containers.

- Provide purses and a box or till containing 1p coins. Show the children how to select and pay for the goods. Participate in the role play and model language such as 'That'll be 10p altogether,', 'What do I owe you?' and 'Here's your change.'

Communication, Language and Literacy

 Hear and say initial and final sounds in words.

Listening

- Read a story about going shopping (see Resources). Read it a few times and then invite the children to join in with you as you read. Invite them to respond to the story, saying whether they liked it, found it funny and so on. Encourage them to act out the story in the role play area, using the vocabulary of the book. Help them to understand and use appropriate vocabulary, such as 'customer', 'manager', 'shopkeeper' and 'aisle'.

Rhyme

- Share the poem 'What do you want to buy today?' on page 30. Draw attention to the rhyming words. Encourage the children to add more words that rhyme – for example, tie/fly and sauce/horse.

Writing – teacher scribing

- Discuss with the children the names of people who work or shop in a supermarket – customer, manager, checkout assistant and shelf stacker. Model the writing process, explaining letter formation and phonemes, to make badges. The children can wear these badges when they enter the supermarket.

- Discuss with the children the large signs that give information in a supermarket (see Creative Development), indicating which products are in which aisles.

Extension

- Model writing signs as above and ask the more able children to copy them. Add these signs to the display in the role play area.

Independent writing

- Help the children as they make name badges. They should write their full name on a small piece of card. Laminate them and stick a safety pin on the back.

Drama

- Create an incident in the role play area. Take on a role yourself, such as a harassed mother or a grumpy shop assistant. Encourage the children to react in role – for example, speak to one child as if he or she is the shop manager. Make a complaint, such as the lack of an item on the shelf or the delay in the queue at the checkout.

Physical Development

 Handle tools safely and with increasing control. Move with control and coordination.

Cutting skills

See Creative Development.

Movement

- Ask the children to pretend they are walking around the shops. Tell them to vary their movements to show hurrying, browsing, stopping and searching high and low. Create a narrative for them to act out – for example, 'Now your trolley is heavy, so you have to push quite hard. Can you reach that item on the top shelf? Which cereal do you want?' Let them work in pairs and then small groups. Tell them to decide who will be the leader. The leader walks through the supermarket, stopping, looking, selecting items, and so on. The group must mimic their leader.

At the end of this week ask the children to bring to school next week, a tin of food such as baked beans, tuna or tomatoes. Don't be too specific, to ensure variety.

WEEK 2

The role play area

The children will continue to create the supermarket area and use it for role play. They will act out scenarios such as selecting food and paying for it at the checkout, asking assistants for specific items and helping someone who has dropped their shopping. They will make a **delivery lorry**, collect a range of **canned foods** and consider the importance of labels.

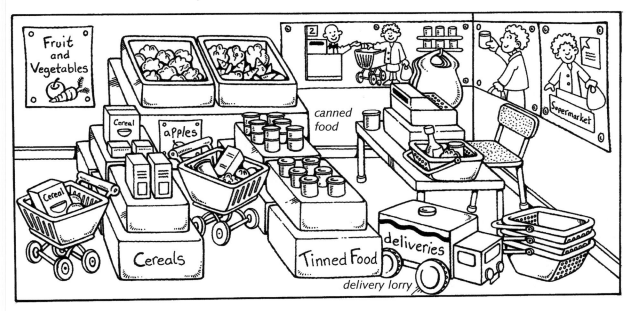

Resources

Photocopiable:

Poems and songs 1 (page 30)

Fiction books:

A Pipkin of Pepper by Helen Cooper, Random House
(0 385600 07 0)
Tom and Pippo Go Shopping by Helen Oxenbury, Atheneum
(0 689712 78 2)
Bear Goes Shopping by Harriet Ziefert, HarperCollins
(0 694000 85 X)
When we go shopping by Nick Butterworth, Little Brown & Co
(0 316119 00 8)
Wilberforce goes shopping by Margaret Gordon, Viking Kestrel
Picture Books (0 670807 01 X)

Music and songs:

Bobby Shaftoe Clap Your Hands by Sue Nicholls, A&C Black
(0 713635 56 8)
Tom Thumb's Musical Maths by Helen MacGregor, A&C Black
(0 713649 71 2)
Junior Choice, Vol. 1, Audio CD, Music for Pleasure (B000026GOS)

Materials

- A 'feely' bag (with either an elasticated or a drawstring opening)
- Real fruit or vegetables – apple, orange, potato, carrot, small cucumber
- Canned foods – for example, baked beans, tuna, fruit salad (children to contribute to this collection)
- Bowl and spoon
- Can-opener
- Slice of bread
- Small boxes – label one 'Orders'
- Lids
- Pictures of delivery lorries
- 1p and 2p coins
- A till roll or strips of paper
- Glue and paint

Personal, Social and Emotional Development

 Respond to significant experiences, showing a range of feelings when appropriate.

Circle time

- ❑ Encourage a discussion that explores feelings about going shopping. Ask questions such as: Have you ever been lost? What did you do? How did you feel? What should you do if you are lost? Who should you talk to?
- ❑ Read *A Pipkin of Pepper* or another story about being lost (see Resources).
- ❑ If possible, play the recording of 'I've Lost My Mummy' by Rolf Harris (see Resources).

Mathematical Development

 Use developing mathematical ideas and methods to solve practical problems.

Music and song

- ❑ Sing the song 'Supermarket Shop' from *Bobby Shaftoe Clap Your Hands* (see Resources).
- ❑ Sing the song 'Mystery Bag' from *Tom Thumb's Musical Maths* (see Resources).

Shapes

- ❑ Use the collection of cans brought in, and ask children to stack them carefully on a shelf or table. Talk about the shape of the cans. Ask the following questions: Why can't you stack them on their sides? Can you stack them in a pattern? How many can you stack safely? (This could be practised on the floor.) Give the children a large box and ask them to stack the tins in the box. How many tins did they manage to place in the box without any showing over the top of the box? Encourage them to try different ways of stacking the tins.
- ❑ Ask the children to draw the pattern of stacked cans on individual whiteboards. Number them.

Number work

- ❑ Introduce 2p coins. Show the children how one 2p coin has the same value as two 1p coins.
- ❑ In the supermarket, model using 2p and 1p coins. Ask the children to buy items using both coins.

Extension

- ❑ Encourage more able children to record prices on the till roll to give as receipts.

Communication, Language and Literacy

 Use talk to organise, sequence and clarify thinking, ideas, feelings and events.

Poems and rhymes

- ❑ Select a poem from page 30 and recite it to the children. Let them join in with you and aim for them to know the poem by heart by the end of the week.
- ❑ Point out the rhyming words and invite children to think of other rhyming words – for example, sweets/streets/meats/beats/feasts/seats/treats/; tray/play/day/bay/may/say/stay/pay/way.

Listening

- ❑ Read a story from the suggested fiction list (or a similar book) and invite the children to join in with you as you read.

Language development

- ❑ Play 'What is it?' Show and name all the pieces of fruit and the vegetables and then place one of them into the feely bag without the children seeing. Tell them to sit in a circle. If possible, sing the song: 'A Feely Game' from *Bobby Shaftoe Clap Your Hands* (see Resources) or use a recording of lively music. As the children are singing, they should pass the bag around. At the end of the song, the child holding the bag puts his hand into it and tries to identify the object. He should describe it to the class. 'It feels hard. It has bumps all over it.'
- ❑ Play the shopping basket memory game. Ask a small group of children to sit in a circle. Start off: 'I went to the shops today and I bought an apple.' The first

child should repeat what you have said and add another item – for example, 'I went to the shops today and I bought an apple and a loaf of bread.' Continue round the circle with each child adding an extra item. How many items can they remember?

Teacher modelling – making a shopping list

❏ Model for the children writing lists. Explain how we write the items one under the other and cross each one off as we buy the item. Talk about starting each item with a capital letter. Demonstrate how you use sounds to help you to spell the different items – for example, butter, milk, bread.

❏ Some of the children may be able to try to write their own lists.

I ned
ChcoLt
I ned
Swets
I ned
apples
I ned
c[ts
I ned
origes
I ned
Bred

I ned
FishFigs
BttSand
I ned
Chies

Extension

❏ Ask the more able children to tell you how many sounds they can hear in the words.

Writing labels

❏ Show the children the labels on different cans. Draw the cans on the board and model writing the labels. Discuss initial phonemes and letter formation.

Independent writing

❏ Invite the children to make lists of items to be ordered for the supermarket. These orders could be placed in a special 'orders box'.

❏ Draw some outlines of different cans and ask the children to design labels for them. They can draw pictures, copy labels or attempt their own writing.

Knowledge and Understanding of the World

 Investigate objects and materials by using all of their senses as appropriate.

Food labels

❏ Set up a table, preferably in the role play area, and display a small selection of canned foods with the labels removed. (Use a permanent marker to initial the base of each can so that you can use any unopened cans!) Have ready a slice of bread, a bowl, a spoon and a can-opener. Wear an apron and/or a chef's hat. Collect the cans of food brought in by the children. Look at and discuss the labels. Ask questions such as: How do you know what is inside this can? What could happen if there was no label? Tell the children that you are going to make beans on toast. Toast a slice of bread in the toaster. Show them the unlabelled cans. Ask a child to come up and select a can that they think contains baked beans. Open it and pour over the toast. Did the child choose the right can? Repeat this activity to make a fruit salad.

Creative Development

 Express and communicate their ideas and thoughts by using a widening range of materials.

Physical Development

 Move with confidence and imagination.

Bar codes and delivery lorries

❏ Look at the bar codes on some of the cans. Explain their purpose and the place of IT in the supermarket. Explain that bar codes are accurate and make going through the checkout quicker.

❏ Provide a selection of thick and thin felt-tipped pens and ask the children to create their own bar codes. Display these in the supermarket.

❏ Talk about how goods are brought to the supermarket. Ask the following questions: Have you seen the big lorries on the roads or arriving at (local supermarket)? How do you know which shop they are going to? How are the lorries unloaded? Ask the children to draw and paint pictures of the lorries being unloaded.

❏ Provide a selection of boxes, lids, glue and paint. Ask the children to make a delivery lorry. (NB: it is a good idea to turn the boxes inside out beforehand to make them easier to paint.) Display the vehicles in or around the supermarket.

The beans game

❏ Tell the children to stand in a circle. Explain the actions for each bean:

Broad beans: stand with feet and arms wide apart
French beans: say 'Ooh la la!' and wave hand
String beans: make a tall, narrow shape
Runner beans: run on the spot
Kidney beans: make a curved shape
Jelly beans: wobble
Baked beans: drop to ground in small shape
Frozen beans: freeze!

When you say what kind of bean you want the children to be they are to make the appropriate action.

WEEK 3

The role play area

This week, the children will complete the supermarket with bakery items and will make **bread rolls**. They will role play being market stall holders and persuading customers to buy. They will also explore simple marketing and advertising ideas. Ask the children to cut out advertisements from magazines and bring them to school.

Resources

Photocopiables:

Poems and songs 1 (page 30)
How to make bread rolls (pages 32 and 34)
Ingredients pictures for bread rolls (page 33)

Non-fiction books:

Busy Places: Supermarket, Franklin Watts (0 749645 63 6)
In your neighbourhood – Shopping by Sally Hewitt, Franklin Watts (0 749652 02 0)
Beans on Toast by Paul Dowling, Walker Books (0 744598 36 2)
Star Science: Group Discussion Book (The Bakery), Ginn (0 602267 34 X)
Who Helps Us? – In a Supermarket, 'Little Nippers' series, Heinemann Library (0 431173 23 0)
I Know That! Bread by Clare Llewellyn, Franklin Watts (0 749654 16 3)
A Day in the Life of a Baker, Franklin Watts (0 749641 06 1)

Materials:

- 'Pop to the shops' – a shopping game by GLS Educational Supplies (sales@glsed.co.uk)
- Pictures of advertisements that the children would recognise – for example, for a toy
- 1p, 2p and 5p coins
- Balance scales and gram weights, or other scales if you do not have a balance
- Ingredients for bread rolls (see page 32)
- Baking tray
- Access to an oven
- Plastic cutting/shaping tools
- Dough cutters and salt dough
- Ball

Week 3 – The bakery

Personal, Social and Emotional Development

 Be confident to try new activities, initiate ideas and speak in a familiar group.

Circle time

❑ Ask the children the following questions: When you go into a shop, you see lots of signs and posters. What do they tell you? How else do you know what is in the shops? Talk about television advertisements and magazines. Ask if they have ever been to a market and heard the stall holders calling out. Talk about what they said.

❑ Experiment with 'sales talk'. Say 'Come and buy my juicy oranges.' Ask the children to try shouting it. Who is more likely to get people to come and buy? Make up and try other calls. Try this in the role play supermarket. Discuss how else they could get people to buy in their shop. Talk about posters and advertisements. (Cut prices; Buy one, get one free; Our apples are only …)

Mathematical Development

 In practical activities and discussion, begin to use vocabulary involved in adding and subtracting.

Adding and subtracting

❑ Introduce 5p coins. Show the children how one 5p coin has the same value as five 1p coins.

❑ In the supermarket, model using 5p, 2p and 1p coins. Encourage the children to buy items using these coins.

❑ Read the poem 'Shopping Basket' by Charles Thomson (page 30). Ask the children to work with a partner and to add up the items in the poem.

❑ Play 'Pop to the shops' (see Resources) or any other commercial game that involves adding.

Extension

❑ Investigate using different combinations of coins, such as 2p, 2p and 1p to make 5p. Model, and encourage the children to use this idea in their role play.

Creative Development

 Respond in a variety of ways to what they see, hear, smell, touch and feel.

The bakery

❑ Take groups of children into the role play supermarket. Pretend that you are in the bakery. Ask: What is sold in the bakery department? Have you ever smelled bread being baked in a bakery? Did you like the smell? Have you ever seen an in-store bakery?

Making bread rolls

❑ Tell the children that they are going to make bread rolls (see pages 32 and 33). Help them to weigh the ingredients. Use vocabulary such as 'grams', 'balance', 'more' and 'less' and encourage them to do the same. Explain that it is very dangerous to touch hot bread as it comes out of the oven. The bread has to cool down on a special tray until it is not too hot to touch. When they have cooked the bread and it is cool invite them to have a taste.

Making cakes and biscuits

❑ Make items to sell in the bakery department of your supermarket. Provide large balls of salt dough and some simple shaping tools (for example, plastic knives and cutters). Talk to the children about making cakes, rolls, biscuits and so on. Do this with one group at a time. For example, ask the first group to make fairy cakes and the second group to make biscuits. This will encourage thought about size and scale. Allow to dry thoroughly in a warm oven. Paint then glaze, if you wish, with watered-down PVA glue.

Communication, Language and Literacy

 Enjoy using spoken and written language.

Language development

❑ Introduce vocabulary such as 'cheaper', 'dearer', 'expensive', 'cost', 'consistency' and 'ingredients'.

Phonics

❑ Provide the following – a tin, box, bag, cup, jug, mug, hat and pen. Help the children to identify the phonemes in cvc words. Ask the children how many phonemes they can hear in 'tin'. Write the word on the board and sound out the letters as you write. Repeat with two or three other cvc words. Ask the children to help you sound out the letters as you write the words on the board.

Extension

❑ Ask the children to write the cvc words on individual whiteboards.

Listening

❑ Show the children a non-fiction book about shops and shopping (see Resources). Discuss with them how they know it is not a story. Show them the purpose of the contents list and the index. Ask the children to suggest things they might like to know about a supermarket and demonstrate how you use the contents page and the index. Talk about the illustrations and point out that they are generally photographs. Read a small section from the book. Ask the children if they notice anything about the way the book is written. Leave the reference books in the role play area for the children to look at.

Reading instructions

❑ Tell the children they are going to make a recipe for bread rolls. Using pages 33 and 34, cut out the pictures and instructions. Give out the 'What you need' cards to individual children. Write on the board the title 'Making bread rolls' and then write a subheading 'What you need'. Ask individual children to come out and, using sticky tack, place their 'What you need' cards under the subheading 'What you need'. Then write the subheading 'What to do' on the board. Give out the method cards and ask the children to choose the pictures in the correct order. Continue until all the pictures and text are displayed.

Extension: making recipe cards

❑ Give each child a cut-out copy of page 34. Ask them to put the four steps in the correct order. When they have recreated the recipe, support them as they read the instructions.

Knowledge and Understanding of the World

 Talk about features they like and dislike.

Advertisements

❑ Ask the children to cut out some advertisements from newspapers and magazines and bring them to school. Make a collage of advertisements by sticking them randomly onto a large sheet of paper. Talk about the advertisements. What are they trying to sell? Who would buy the items?

Week 3 – The bakery

Music and song

❏ Sing the 'Supermarket shop' song again from *Bobby Shaftoe Clap Your Hands (See Resources)*. Vary the items in the basket to include items in the advertisements.

Scientific observation

❏ Talk about changes to ingredients when preparing and cooking bread rolls. Ask questions: What happened when you added the yeast? How did the consistency change as you added the water? Did you notice how the colour changed when the dough was cooked? Did you like the smell of the bread as it was baking?

Physical Development

Handle tools, objects and malleable materials safely and with increasing control. Move with confidence, imagination and in safety.

Changing shape – following instructions

❏ Talk to the children about how they changed the shape of the salt dough to make balls when creating their bakery products. Discuss how they rolled it, stretched it and squeezed it. Pretend to take a ball of dough in your hands. Show how big it is. Now squeeze it and push it into a different shape. Roll it into a ball again. This time stretch it and pull it to make a different shape. Tell the children that they are going to be a ball of dough and they are going to change their body shape. Tell them to follow these instructions: 'Make yourself into as round a ball shape as you can. Hold your shape. Now imagine that someone is squeezing and pushing you into a different shape. What shape will you be? Now become a ball shape again. Now imagine that you are being stretched. Show me your new shape.'

Rolling

❏ Talk about how balls can roll across the floor. Show the children a ball rolling. Tell the children to roll like a ball and show you as many ways as they can.

Play the beans game

❏ Play the beans game again from Week 2, but this time speed up the instructions.

At the end of this week, ask the children to collect empty cereal boxes and bring them into school next week.

WEEK 4

The role play area

This week, the children will consolidate their learning in the role play supermarket. It will be a week of investigations in which they will be encouraged to use their imagination in role play and be presented with problem-solving activities.

NB: during this week, show the children how to take digital photographs of their peers playing in the supermarket. These images should be printed out in preparation for making calendars in Week 6.

Resources

Photocopiables:

Poems and songs 1 (page 30)
Food pictures (page 35)

Fiction books:

I went to the Zoopermarket by Nick Sharrett, Scholastic UK
(0 439013 61 5)
The Shopping Basket by John Burningham, Red Fox
(0 099899 30 2)

Music and songs:

The Handy Band by Sue Nicholls, A&C Black (0 713668 97 0)

Materials:

- Shopping list game, GLS Educational Supplies Ltd (sales@glsed.co.uk)
- Ready-made books, such as zigzag or one-cut books
- A ready-made book, 'big book' scale
- Empty and full cereal boxes of varying sizes
- Cup or scoop
- Sand tray containing dry sand
- Range of construction kits containing wheels
- Two apples
- Garden canes
- Newspaper
- Masking tape and/or clear adhesive tape
- Tissue, crepe and drawing paper and parcel tape
- scales
- bags

Personal, Social and Emotional Development

 Have a developing awareness of their own needs, views and feelings and be sensitive to the needs, views and feelings of others.

Turn taking

- ❏ Through the problem-solving activities that the children will do throughout the week, they will learn to express their ideas, communicate with others and negotiate turn taking.
- ❏ Sing the song 'My turn, your turn' from *The Handy Band* (see Resources).

Mathematical Development

 Use developing mathematical ideas and methods to solve practical problems.

Addition and subtraction

- ❏ Introduce 10p coins. Show the children how one 10p coin has the same value as ten x 1p coins.
- ❏ In the supermarket, model using 10p, 5p, 2p and 1p coins. Encourage the children to use them.

Extension

- ❏ Investigate using different combinations of coins to make 10p. Model, and encourage the children to use this idea in their role play.

Problem-solving activities

- ❏ Show the children a full cereal box and a full small box of rice. Ask them to guess which is the heavier. Use scales to check their predictions. Talk about how some big things can be lighter than smaller things.
- ❏ Set up other challenges, such as 'Which is heavier, a bread roll or an apple?'

Weighing

- ❏ In the role play area provide a set of scales, some bags and scoops. Let the children scoop food into the bags and place them on the scales.

Communication, Language and Literacy

 Write … in simple sentences.

Listening

- ❏ Read the poem 'The Corner Shop' (page 30) to the children and invite them to repeat the words after you. When they are confident, ask them to join in with you. Try to lower your voice so that they are saying the words without obvious support. Encourage them to say the words with intonation and expression.

Writing – teacher scribing

- ❏ Make a six-page 'big book'. Tape a piece of card halfway down each page. This will be a 'lift-the-flap'. Scribe the children's ideas of things they could buy in the supermarket at the top of each page – for example, 'I bought a loaf of bread.' Under the flap draw a picture of a loaf of bread. Talk through the writing process as you write. Continue in the same way with other items suggested by the children. Write a title on the cover of the book, such as 'I went to the supermarket'.

Shared reading

- ❏ Read together the completed book, talking about reading from left to right and pointing to the words as you read. Ask if there is anyone who would like to read the book to the class.

Writing – independent

- ❏ Let the children select the form of their own 'I went to the supermarket' book (pages or zigzag) and give them appropriate support as they write their ideas. Some of them will need to go over words written in highlighter, some could copy under your writing, whereas others may feel confident to write independently. Point out the words, labels and captions around the room and role play area to help them. Try to read everyone's book to the class and ask those who are confident to read their own.

Knowledge and Understanding of the World

 Select the tools and techniques they need to shape, assemble and join materials they are using.

Problem-solving activities

❑ In the role play supermarket, set up a table with different types of paper – tissue, crepe, newspaper, good quality drawing or cartridge paper and parcel paper. Provide glues, a stapler, scissors, pencils and adhesive tapes (masking and clear tape). Ask the children to make a shopping bag strong enough to carry a can of baked beans. Explain that their bag must have a handle.

Outside activity

❑ Provide a range of construction kits that include wheels, such as Mobilo or Lego. Ask the children to construct a vehicle that can transport things to the supermarket – for example, two apples. Have starting and finishing points to test the vehicles.

❑ Provide a selection of materials, such as garden canes, masking tape, newspaper, a couple of chairs and a length of fabric. Ask the children to build something for the supermarket. Leave this activity totally open-ended and observe their response.

Creative Development

 Use their imagination in drama and role play.

Drama – creating a tableau

❑ Revisit movements from Week 1 (walking, hurrying, browsing, reaching and searching high and low). Remind the children of the different people who might be in the supermarket. Practise these movements again. Practise freezing these movements.

❑ Divide the children into groups (about six children in each group). Ask the groups to decide what each individual will be doing in an imaginary photo of shoppers. Tell the children to practise their tableau.

Visit each group to give support. When everyone is ready, invite each group to show their tableau to the rest of the class.

Digital photos

❑ If possible, help the children to take a digital photograph of each group for turning into calendars in Week 6.

Painting

❑ Ask the children to paint pictures of a group of people at the supermarket. Display these around the classroom.

Drama

❑ Encourage role play in the supermarket. Create a dynamic situation – for example, someone has lost their purse or someone takes someone else's trolley. Increase the depth of role play through adult support. Encourage the children to use the vocabulary they have met during this unit.

Physical Development

 Show awareness of space, of themselves and of others.

Play the shopping department game

❑ Make two copies of the food pictures on page 35. Stick one set in different parts of the hall or classroom. Hold the matching pictures behind your back. Tell the children to 'go shopping' and choose a corner to go to. They should pretend to browse along the aisle and scan the shelves. Randomly select a picture from behind your back and hold it up. Those children who are by that picture are out. Bring the remaining children back to the centre of the room and repeat until there is a winner.

At the end of this week, tell the class that they are going to transform the supermarket into a toy shop. Ask them to bring in a soft toy to put on the shelf.

At the shops

WEEK 5

The role play area

During this week, the children will decide how to rearrange the role play area to make a toy shop. They must decide where the boxes will go and where to place the till. They will then make **decorations**, **3-D cards** and **junk model toys**. The children will become familiar with the story of the Nativity and learn how and why Christians celebrate Christmas.

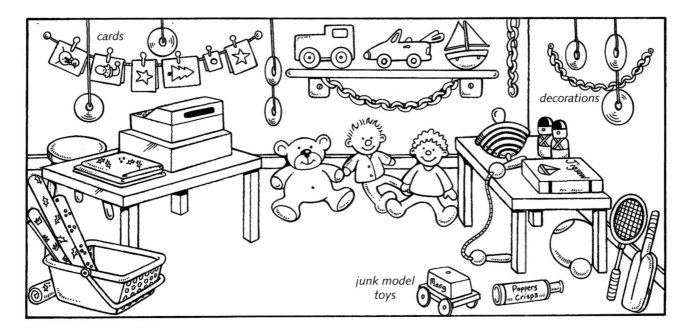

Resources

Photocopiable:

Poems and songs 2 (page 31)

Books:

The Christmas Gift: the story of the nativity by Elizabeth Laird, Scholastic (0 439981 43 3)
This is the star by Joyce Dunbar and Gary Blythe, Doubleday (0 385406 02 9)
The Nativity Play by Nick Butterworth and Mick Inkpen, Hodder (0 340398 94 9)
The Donkey's Christmas Song by Nancy Tafuri, Scholastic (0 439273 13 7)

Materials:

- Selection of soft toys
- Selection of toys such as a hoop, car, yoyo, doll or ball
- Paper strips or ready-made strips for making paper chains
- Paints
- Corks, or other suitable objects, for printing
- Green card cut into simple template of a Christmas tree
- Green card or firm green paper
- Card cut and folded into the size and shape of a greetings card
- Strip of draught excluder
- Silver sprinkle stars or shapes
- Junk materials

Audiovisual:

- BBC Festivals Video 'Christmas' (BBC Publications)

Music and songs:

- *Bingo Lingo* by Helen Macgregor, A&C Black (0 713650 75 3)
- Tape or CD of Christmas carols

Personal, Social and Emotional Development

 Have a developing respect for their own cultures and beliefs and those of others.

The Christmas story

❏ Tell the story of the first Christmas. Watch a video of the Christmas story (see Resources).

Giving

❏ Discuss with the class the gifts brought by the shepherds and the three Wise Men for the baby Jesus. Talk about gifts they or other people they know have given and for what occasions. Ask the children why we give presents. Talk about how it feels to give someone a present, the pleasure of giving and receiving, of being loved and valued.

Sharing

❏ Sing 'Hey Little Playmate' from *Bingo Lingo* (see Resources). If possible, write the words on a large sheet of paper or on an OHT. Point at the words as you sing and encourage the children to join in with them.

Creative Development

 Explore colour, texture and shape in two or three dimensions.

Making a toy shop

❏ Explain to the children that they are going to turn their supermarket into a toy shop for Christmas. Ask them how they think the boxes should be arranged to represent the shelves. Invite them to place their soft toys on the shelves. Where should the till be placed? Who do they think will visit the toy shop? How many assistants will they need?

Decorating the toy shop

❏ Make decorations for the shop using CDs suspended from the ceiling and paper chains made by the children. Display these around the shop.

Wrapping gifts

❏ Place a pile of wrapping paper near the till for the assistant to wrap up the presents (see Mathematical Development).

Making 'junk' toys

❏ Ask the children to each make a toy to sell. This is an open-ended task and they can make whatever they wish, using a selection of boxes and other 'junk' materials, glue and paint. Encourage them to write a price tag for their toy.

Making a window display

❏ Suggest the children make a window display for the toy shop. This could be by arranging toys on or around a box near the 'door' of the shop or by painting pictures of their toys.

Making 3-D Christmas cards

❑ Taking the theme 'Christmas in the shop', show the children how to cut round a simple Christmas tree template on firm green paper or light card and tell them to cut out two identical trees. Mount the first tree on a folded greetings card. Place a small strip of foam draught excluder on the tree and stick the second tree on top. Then decorate the tree with stars and glitter shapes.

Mathematical Development

 Talk about, recognise and recreate simple patterns.

IT Roamer

❑ Fix a small box to the top of the Roamer. Show the children how to programme the Roamer a given distance, forwards and backwards. Place a small toy in the box and ask the children to programme the Roamer to take the toy from one child to another.

Sequential patterns

❑ Prepare sheets of paper, paint and corks or other objects for printing. Show the children how to make a sequential pattern. Count the number of different shapes in the pattern and then explain that after a predetermined number you start again and repeat the pattern. You could ask them to repeat the pattern using a different colour. Ask the children to create sequential patterns and designs, to create wrapping paper.

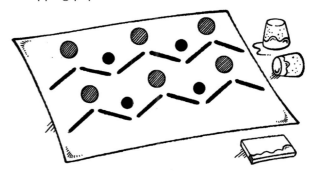

Extension

❑ Play 'Copy my numbers.' Say a number, for example 3, and ask the child to repeat it. Then repeat the 3 and add another number, for example 7. Ask the child to repeat the two numbers in the correct order. How many numbers can the child remember?

Communication, Language and Literacy

 Explore and experiment with sounds, words and texts.

Circle time

❑ Talk about giving. Ask the children to express their ideas and feelings, to listen to others and take turns in conversation – for example, 'I would like to give my mum a … because …'

Listening

❑ Read a story about Christmas from the suggested list (or similar). Discuss the story and the illustrations with the children. If possible, ask them to join in with the retelling.

❑ Select one of the Christmas poems (page 31) and discuss it with the children.

❑ Teach them the carol 'Away in a manger' (page 31).

Writing – teacher scribing

❑ Discuss with the children the different notices they can see in shops (for example, 'Bargain Buys', 'All these toys for under £1', 'Please queue from this end', 'Please do not touch' and 'Please pay here'). Explain that they are going to help you to make notices to place in the role play area. Ask them what notices they would like in their shop and demonstrate how to write them.

Extension

❑ Invite more able children to make some of their own notices. Display them in the role play area.

Knowledge and Understanding of the World

Find out about their environment and talk about features they like or dislike.

Shopping at Christmas

❑ Talk about busy streets. Discuss with the children how at Christmas time the streets are very busy and full of people seeking to buy food and presents. Ask the following questions: Why are shops decorated at Christmas? Do you like going shopping when the streets are full of people? What do you dislike about shopping at Christmas time? Do you like Christmas decorations? Which do you like best? What special food do you buy at Christmas time?

Physical Development

Move with control and coordination.

Music and movement

❑ Remind the children about the story of Christmas. Play the carol 'How far is it to Bethlehem?' Talk about the way Mary and Joseph had to walk a long way to Bethlehem. Ask the children to move around the hall slowly and quietly. Then ask them to show you how the shepherds would have moved when they heard the news of the birth of Jesus. Ask them

to tiptoe into the stable so that they would not wake the baby. Finally, they should stride across the room like the Wise Men and kneel to offer their gifts.

❑ Create a narrative about a Christmas shopping trip and ask the children to move around according to your story. For example, 'First you are waiting at the bus stop looking out for the bus. Now you are stepping up into the bus...' and so on. Explain that they are going to pretend to collect some presents. Tell them to reach up high for a present from a top shelf, to bend down for a present on a low shelf and so on. Ask them to walk back home pretending to carry all the shopping.

At the shops

The role play area

This week, the children are going to visit the toy shop and meet Father Christmas. They will write letters to him. They will make more decorations, calendars and gifts, and Christmas biscuits to decorate and eat.

Resources

Photocopiables:

Christmas poems and songs (page 31)
Christmas biscuits (page 32)

Fiction books:

Tosca's Christmas by Anne Mortimer, Puffin (0 140548 40 8)
Christmas present by John Burningham, Walker Books
(0 744525 74 8)
Is that you, Father Christmas? by Siobhan Dodds, Walker Books
(0 744594 28 6)

Non-fiction book:

My Christmas, 'Little Nippers' series, Heinemann Library
(0 431186 32 4)

Music and songs:

Tom Thumb's Musical Maths by Helen MacGregor, A&C Black
(0 713649 71 2)

Materials:

- Large box or tub (for a bran tub) – for example, a clean waste bin
- Shredded paper
- Selection of small toys
- Digital photographs taken in Week 4
- Calendar tabs
- Tissue paper and small items of collage materials such as sequins and beads
- Coloured discs of card
- Wool or string for hanging the discs
- Coin-shaped sweets or mints
- Double-sided tape
- Masking tape
- Ingredients for Christmas biscuits
- Christmas biscuit cutters
- Small boxes
- Sheets of newsprint
- Wavy-cut scissors
- Bauble templates – for example, circles, stars, moon, snowman, Christmas tree
- Father Christmas outfit for a child

Personal, Social and Emotional Development

 Respond to significant experiences, showing a range of feelings when appropriate.

Circle time

❏ Ask the children: What makes you excited? Are you excited about Christmas? Do you think grown-ups get excited about Christmas?

❏ Talk about people who might be lonely at Christmas – old people and those who have no homes.

❏ Pass around the circle a large bowl and a wooden spoon. Ask each child in turn to 'stir the pudding' and make a secret Christmas wish.

Mathematical Development

 Use developing mathematical ideas and methods to solve practical problems.

Problem-solving – wrapping parcels

❏ Provide a selection of small boxes, masking tape and sheets of newsprint. Ask the children to work in pairs to try wrapping the boxes.

Fitting boxes into a shape

❏ Give the children a selection of boxes of different sizes – for example, a wine box, shoe box, egg box and empty matchbox. Tape up all the boxes except the largest, so that the children do not put them inside each other. Ask them to see how many boxes they can put inside the largest box. They should try packing the boxes in different ways.

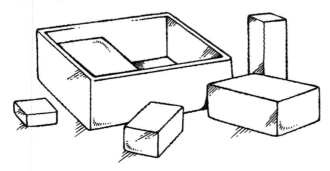

❏ Sing the song 'Which shapes?' from *Tom Thumb's Musical Maths* (See Resources).

Extension

❏ Tell the children that the shopkeeper can fit eight toys on his shelf. If he has put six toys on the shelf, how many more can he fit? Repeat with other numbers and write the figures as a sum, for example $6 + 2 = 8$.

Communication, Language and Literacy

 Attempt writing for different purposes, using features of different forms, such as lists.

Modelled writing

❏ Tell the children that they are going to write to Father Christmas and ask him what he would like for Christmas. Show them how to write a letter. Write the school address at the top and talk about adding the date. Demonstrate how to start your letter and what to write. 'Dear Father Christmas, We would like to know what you would like as a present. We hope you have a happy Christmas. Love from …'

❏ Discuss with the children what they think Father Christmas would like and make a list of their suggestions.

Extension

❏ Encourage some of the children to add to the list during the day.

Shared reading

❏ Write a reply from Father Christmas and show it to the class the following day. You might add in some of the suggestions that the children have made. Talk about writing thank you letters.

Rhyming songs

❏ Sing 'Hey Little Playmate' from *Bingo Lingo* (See Resources). Omit the rhyming words and ask the children to predict them.

Drama

❏ Invite the children to get into role as one of the following: Santa, a parent or a child. Make a bran tub for Santa's grotto by filling a large container with, for example, shredded paper, and hiding in it some small toys from the toy shop. Tell the children to dip into the bran tub for a 'gift' when they visit Santa in the toy shop. Tell them to keep the gift hidden from Santa while they describe it. Challenge Santa to guess what it is. For example, 'It has four wheels. It has windows. It has a steering wheel.' (A car) Encourage dialogue between all the characters. For example, 'Ooh, what a lovely present! You are so lucky!' and 'Thank you Santa.'

Singing

❏ Sing 'The twelve days of Christmas' with the class.

Independent writing

❏ Help the children to write a greeting in their Christmas tree card. Write in highlighter pen for those who need help so they can write over it. Ask others to copy from a card.

Knowledge and Understanding of the World

Observe, find out about and identify features in the place they live and the natural world.

Christmas trees

❏ Talk to the children about different Christmas trees – real and artificial. Ask the children: Do you or will you have a Christmas tree at home? Will it be a real or artificial one? Do you know where Christmas trees come from? Do Christmas trees lose their leaves in winter like some other types of tree do? In which season of the year is Christmas celebrated? Be sensitive towards children of other cultures and religions. Allow them to compare and talk about their symbols and customs.

Creative Development

Use their imagination in art and design.

Calendars

❏ Using the digital photos of role play in the supermarket from Week 4, ask the children to mount them on card and decorate the borders as they wish. Add calendar tabs and hanging ribbon or string.

Design postage stamps for letters to Santa

❏ Using wavy-cut scissors, cut out small squares of paper. Invite the children to design a stamp. Encourage them to add the price – for example, 10p.

Making decorations

❏ Prepare a selection of bauble templates. Ask the children to select a shape, draw round it, cut it out and decorate it on both sides. Ask the children to punch a hole at the top using a hole punch. An adult could thread the hole with wool or decorative string.

Santa's grotto

❏ Have an area in the toy shop designated for Santa. Decorate the grotto with lights and baubles and, if possible, a Christmas tree.

Making gifts

❏ Provide brightly coloured discs of card and some foil-wrapped chocolate coins. Ask the children to punch a hole at the top of the discs and use coloured wool to make a loop. Using double-sided tape, stick a chocolate on each side of the cardboard in the centre of the disc. Let the children take these home to decorate their own homes.

❏ Make Christmas biscuits (see page 32).

(see page 32)

Physical Development

Handle tools safely and with increasing control.

Fine motor skills

❏ Cutting skills – see Creative Development.

Movement

❏ Tell the children to get into groups of three. Two children are to be Santa's reindeer and one is to be Santa. Tell them to pretend they are going from house to house with the presents. Tell the children to trot round the hall. When you ask them to stop, Santa should get out of his sleigh and take up his big bag of presents. He must then mime climbing down the chimney and leaving a present in the room.

❏ Tell the children to sit in a circle. Give one child a small wrapped box and ask him or her to walk round the outside of the circle while the rest of the group sing to the tune of Frère Jacques:

> *Father Christmas (x2)*
> *Here he comes (x2)*
> *Stop and leave a present (x2)*
> *Now he runs (x2)*

Father Christmas drops a present behind one child and hurries on round the circle. The child with the present runs round the circle after Father Christmas. Father Christmas sits down in the space left by the child and the 'new' Father Christmas walks round the circle while the rest sing as before.

Review and evaluation

Encourage the children to reflect on the topic. What have they enjoyed learning about? Which part has been most exciting? Which stories and songs do they remember? Which artwork did they most enjoy doing?

What do you want to buy today?

What do you want to buy today?
What do you want to buy?
A pear for a bear?
A cake for a snake?
A coat for a goat?
Is that what you want to buy?

What do you want to buy today?
What do you want to buy?
A hat for a cat?
A box for a fox?
A house for a mouse?
Is that what you want to buy?

Dee Reid

The Wrong Trolley

Mum, there's cat food in the trolley
And we haven't got a cat!
There's a big bag of potatoes
And we didn't load up that.
Do you remember loading beans
Or peas or cauliflowers?
Mum, I know we're pushing it
But is this trolley ours?

Eric Finney

Shopping Basket

I bought two loaves of bread.
I bought one piece of meat.
I bought three big green apples.
I bought one sticky sweet.
I bought one custard pie.
How many things did I buy?

Charles Thomson

The Corner Shop

It sells apples, green and red,
It sells poppadoms and bread,
It sells comics, it sells coffee,
It sells envelopes and toffee,
It sells carrots, it sells cheese,
It sells stamps and frozen peas,
It sells noodles, it sells string,
It sells every single thing.

Richard James

Going to the shops

(To the tune of 'Daddy's taking us to the zoo tomorrow')

Mum's taking us to the shops tomorrow, shops tomorrow, shops tomorrow
Mum's taking us to the shops tomorrow.
Think of all the things we'll buy.
Fruit and vegetables and soup in the trolley
Cheese and milk and yogurt in the trolley
Bread and biscuits and cakes in the trolley
Look at all the things we've bought.

Dad's taking us to the shops tomorrow, shops tomorrow, shops tomorrow
Dad's taking us to the shops tomorrow.
Think of all the things we'll buy.
Nuts and bolts and nails in the trolley
Spanner and hammer and screws in the trolley
Plugs and bulbs and fuses in the trolley
Look at all the things we've bought.

Gran's taking us to the shops tomorrow, shops tomorrow, shops tomorrow
Gran's taking us to the shops tomorrow.
Think of all the things we'll buy.
Sweets and crisps and ice cream in the trolley
Books and CDs and videos in the trolley
Toys and teddies and games in the trolley
Look at all the things we've bought.

Dee Reid

Away in a manger

Away in a manger, no crib for a bed
The little lord Jesus laid down his sweet head,
The stars in the bright sky looked down where
   he lay
The little lord Jesus asleep on the hay.

The cattle are lowing, the baby awakes
But little lord Jesus no crying he makes.
I love thee Lord Jesus! Look down from the sky,
And stay by my bedside till morning is nigh.

Be near me, Lord Jesus; I ask thee to stay
Close by me for ever, and love me, I pray
Bless all the dear children in thy tender care,
And fit us for heaven to live with thee there.

If I were Father Christmas

If I were Father Christmas
I'd deliver all my toys
By rocket ship, a sleigh's too short
For eager girls and boys,
I'd nip down every chimney-pot
And never miss a roof,
While Rudolf worked the ship's controls
With antler tip and hoof.

Richard Edwards

Christmas

C is for carols we sing Christmas night
h is for holly with berries red bright
r is for reindeer who stand in the snow
i is for icing with silvery glow
s is for Santa who comes very late
t is for tree that stands tall and straight
m is for mincepies I have for tea
a is for angel on top of the tree
s is for stocking I open at dawn
Christmas is coming
The day Christ was born

Brenda Williams

Long, long ago

Wind through the olive trees
Softly did blow,
Round little Bethlehem
Long, long ago.

Sheep on the hillside
Whiter than snow
Shepherds were watching them
Long, long ago.

Then from the happy sky
Angels bent low
Singing their songs of joy
Long, long ago.

For in a manger bed
Cradled we know,
Christ came to Bethlehem
Long, long ago.

Anon

Recipes

Recipe for making bread rolls

You will need

3g (half a sachet) quick action yeast

1 dessertspoon vegetable oil

210ml warm water

Large pinch of salt

350g strong white flour

What to do

1. Set the oven at 230°C / 450°F / Gas mark 8.
2. Put the flour, yeast and salt in a mixing bowl.
3. Add the vegetable oil and water.
4. Mix everything together into a firm dough. Add a little flour if the dough is too sticky, or water if it is too dry.
5. Put the dough on a floured table. Knead it for five minutes by pushing your hands into the dough, gathering it into a ball and turning it repeatedly.
6. Shape the dough into eight rolls.
7. Put the rolls onto a greased baking tray and leave them in a warm place.
8. When the rolls have doubled in size, bake them in the oven for – minutes. They are done if they sound hollow when tapped underneath.
9. Put the rolls onto a wire rack to cool.

How to make Christmas biscuits

You will need

350g plain flour

1 tsp bicarbonate of soda

2 tsp ground ginger

1 tsp ground cinnamon

110g butter – diced

175g soft light brown sugar

4 tbsp golden syrup

1 egg – beaten

What to do

1. Preheat oven to 190°C / 375°F / Gas mark 5.
2. Mix flour, bicarbonate of soda, ginger and cinnamon in a bowl. Rub in butter until mix resembles fine breadcrumbs. Stir in sugar. Add egg and syrup and mix. With fingers, draw into a smooth dough. Knead well. Roll, half at a time, on a floured surface until about 1cm thick.
3. Use Christmas shaped cutters to cut out biscuits. Place on baking parchment on baking trays. Bake for about 12–15 minutes until golden brown. Leave on baking sheets to cool slightly, then transfer to wire racks to cool completely.
4. Decorate with coloured writing icing and/or cake decorations. Alternatively, make a card template (for example, a holly leaf), place the template over each biscuit and sprinkle with icing sugar. Remove template to reveal holly leaf pattern.

'What you need' cards

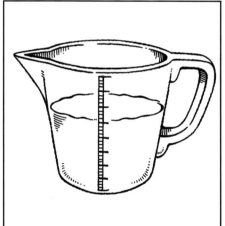

Photocopiable

Bread rolls

Making bread rolls

You will need:
sachet of yeast
vegetable oil
warm water
salt
flour

What to do:

Put the ingredients into a bowl. 	Mix everything together. 
Knead the dough and shape it into rolls. 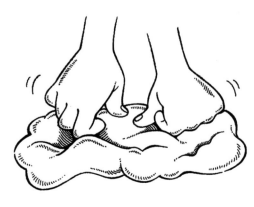	Put the rolls in the oven. 

Bread

Fruit and vegetables

Cereals

Fish

Observational Assessment Chart

Unit: _____

Class: _____

Date: _____

Name	Personal, Social and Emotional Development	Communication, Language and Literacy	Knowledge & Under-standing of the World	Mathematical Development	Creative Development	Physical Development
	Y B G ELG	Y B G ELG	Y B G ELG	Y B G ELG	Y B G ELG	Y B G ELG
	Y B G ELG	Y B G ELG	Y B G ELG	Y B G ELG	Y B G ELG	Y B G ELG
	Y B G ELG	Y B G ELG	Y B G ELG	Y B G ELG	Y B G ELG	Y B G ELG
	Y B G ELG	Y B G ELG	Y B G ELG	Y B G ELG	Y B G ELG	Y B G ELG
	Y B G ELG	Y B G ELG	Y B G ELG	Y B G ELG	Y B G ELG	Y B G ELG
	Y B G ELG	Y B G ELG	Y B G ELG	Y B G ELG	Y B G ELG	Y B G ELG
	Y B G ELG	Y B G ELG	Y B G ELG	Y B G ELG	Y B G ELG	Y B G ELG
	Y B G ELG	Y B G ELG	Y B G ELG	Y B G ELG	Y B G ELG	Y B G ELG
	Y B G ELG	Y B G ELG	Y B G ELG	Y B G ELG	Y B G ELG	Y B G ELG
	Y B G ELG	Y B G ELG	Y B G ELG	Y B G ELG	Y B G ELG	Y B G ELG
	Y B G ELG	Y B G ELG	Y B G ELG	Y B G ELG	Y B G ELG	Y B G ELG
	Y B G ELG	Y B G ELG	Y B G ELG	Y B G ELG	Y B G ELG	Y B G ELG
	Y B G ELG	Y B G ELG	Y B G ELG	Y B G ELG	Y B G ELG	Y B G ELG

Circle the relevant Stepping Stones (Y = Yellow; B = Blue; G = Green or ELG = Early Learning Goal) and write a positive comment as evidence of achievement.

Photocopiable